From the Editor:

Emerald Ent magazine, is a magazine made for the people of Artistry Music, Business, Marketing and Promotions companys alike. feel free to contact, network, or aquire anyone in this publication for their services or products they may have to offer. Marketing is the building of a relationship between a company, a product, and a consumer by understanding the value of their needs." Naturally if those marketing do not understand the value of their product in relation to the customer's needs, then will fail.

The marketing concept is the philosophy that firms should analyze the needs of their customers and then make decisions to satisfy those needs, better than the competition. Today most firms have adopted the marketing concept, but this has not always been the case.

The marketing mix is a crucial tool to help understand what the product or service can offer and how to plan for a successful product offering. The marketing mix is most commonly executed through the 4 P's of marketing: Price, Product, Promotion, and Place. Marketing is the promotion of business products or services to a target audience. ... Common examples of marketing at work include television commercials, billboards on the side of the road, and magazine advertisements. But not all businesses approach the need to market their goods and services the same way.

ISBN-13: 978-1982061272
ISBN-10: 1982061278

c.p. 2017 by R.R.P.

Cover and Back cover designed by: R, Caldwell
Editing and Layout design by: SelectaRoc
Published by: Recording R.O.C. Productions
Magazine setup by: Roc

All rights reserved. No part may be reproduced in any form without permission from the publishers, except by a reviewer who may quote passeges or show in news paper, magazine, or blog.

Elijah H. Mu'ied

Spoken word Artist, Poetry, Actor, Model
www.instagram.com/emuied

Aries rochelle:

Singer, Actress, Security, Ceo
Krocnradio@yahoo.com

"BAD LIKE MIKE"

www.store.cdbaby.com/cd/selectaroc1

Dubbtation Lioness **Dee Jones** **SelectaRoc**

Dubbtation Lioness

Recording Artist, Model, Actress
rashonieka.wilson@gmail.com

New Hit Comin Soon To..........

iTune$ - $potify - Amazon MP3 - Pandora & More......

"get it"

JuicyLena Feat: SelectaRoc

RocTography

Valena "JuicyLena" Wilson

Rapper, Actress, Model, Singer, Music Producer
juicydidit@gmail.com

Shaunnie Bee:
Actress, Model, Singer, Rapper
www.Rocsmovie.com

Sensational Sherry T:

Recording artist, Karaokee Hostess, Catering
sherryt03@yahoo.com

KROCN TV

Fresh Unda-Ground Hype

A variety of specially designed ground transportation services are prearranged and available to satisfy the needs of our clients. The following list of services is currently offered:

- Proms & Formals
- Night Life or Night in town
- Sports Events
- Corporate Events
- Bachelor Parties
- Airport Transportation
- Wedding Transportation
- Wine Tours
- Birthday Parties

7 PASS Lincoln Towncar Limo $50hr

Lyric

Youtube: Lyric Thewebseries

Rubi Pearl
Wholesale Virgin Hair Store & Salon

Bundles **360's**

12" – $55 & up	
14" – $60 & up	
16" – $65 & up	**Custom Colors**
18" – $70 & up	
20" – $75 & up	
22" – $80 & up	**Curly Kinky Curly**
24" – $85 & up	
26" – $90 & up	
28" – $95 & up	
30" – $110 & up	

TEXTURES
Body Wave, Loose, Deep, Curly, Kinky

Frontals   Closures

** 4pk Bundles Package Deals **

11805 Renton ave so, Suite A
Seattle, Wa. 98178 206-384-3571

"Shut Tha Doe"
Performer, Comedian, Karaoke Host, Actor
Darnell Parker - Shutthadoe@gmail.com

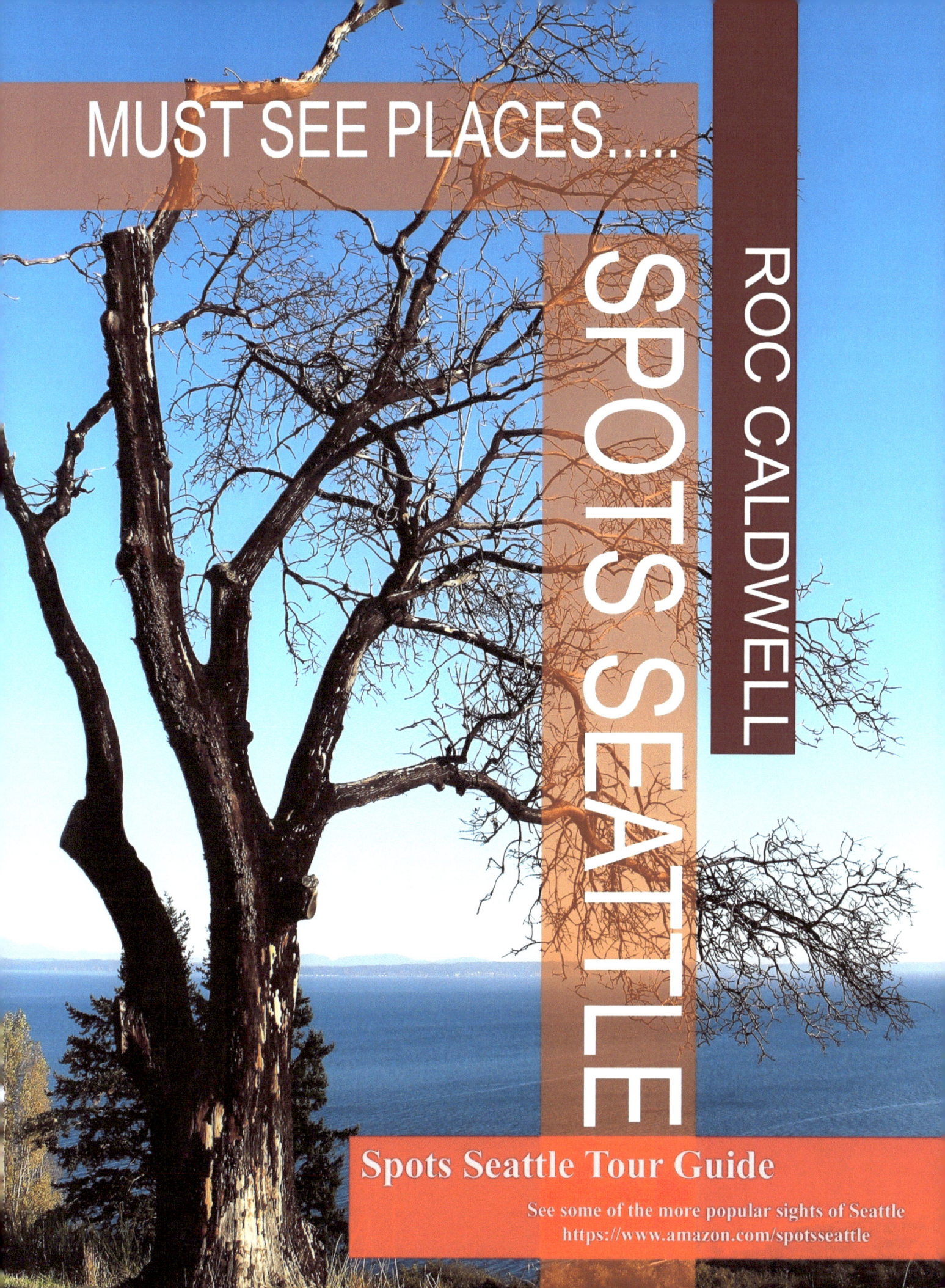

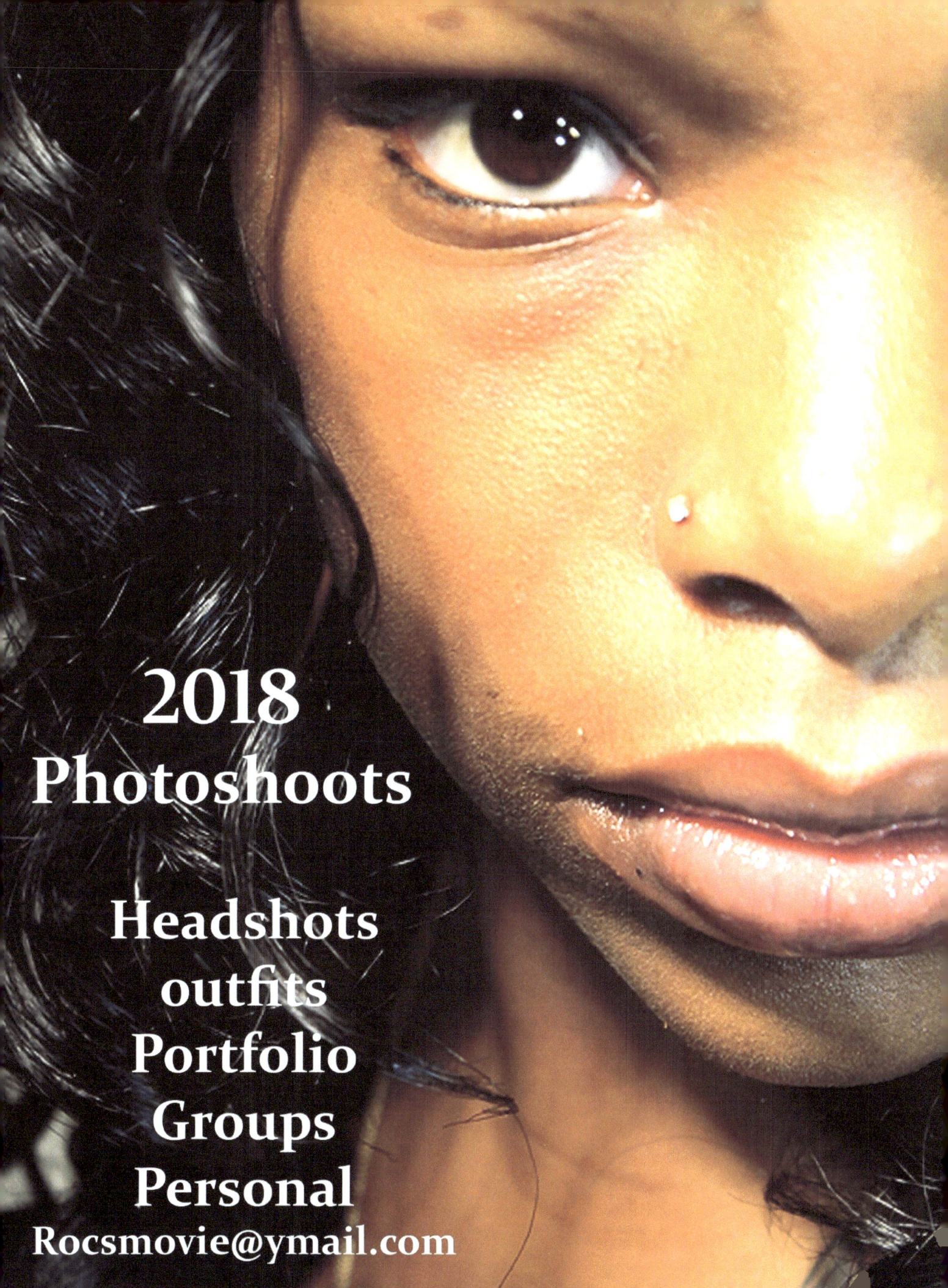

www.ingramcontent.com/pod-product-compliance
Lightning Source LLC
Chambersburg PA
CBHW051831210526
45473CB00005B/1821